The
Final Act

The Final Act

Reflections on Easter

Tony Bower

kevin mayhew

First published in 2002 by KEVIN MAYHEW LTD
Buxhall, Stowmarket, Suffolk, IP14 3BW
E-mail: info@kevinmayhewltd.com

9 8 7 6 5 4 3 2 1 0

ISBN 1 84003 986 8
Catalogue No. 1500547

Cover design by Jonathan Stroulger
Edited and typeset by Matt Lockwood
Printed and bound in Great Britain

Contents

For Claire and Joseph
with all my love

Photo: Tina Luke

About the author

Tony Bower is a full-time Christian Schools Worker for NISCU (Northern Interschools Christian Union), a published author and a regular writer for Scripture Union's SALT magazine for 11-13s.

Tony was born and bred in Barnsley, South Yorkshire, and now lives in a small rural village in North Lancashire. Tony became a Christian when he was 17 and one thing that hasn't changed in 20 years is his desire to share the Gospel message. Other things have changed over time, including the hairline!

He is married to Claire who adores the ground he walks on but wishes he would clean his shoes more often. They have one son, Joseph, who is a song composer, storyteller and performer, usually before the sun has time to wake up. He is 5 years old.

Introduction

This reflection can be used in a variety of ways:

- personal read
- resource for performance pieces
- stimulus for group discussion.

Whichever and however many ways you use the material I pray that the most amazing and dramatic stories of the first Easter will explode from the page and into the lives of all readers and hearers of this book. May God richly bless your read.

TONY

The final act

The drama draws to its finale. The performers are ready, the action is about to begin. Only, this is no play and there are no actors. This is the real thing: a drama destined from the beginning, a production that has long been in the planning, and now the spotlight is shining. There have been no rehearsals – there can't be. It is going to be a once-in-a-lifetime performance. Jesus knows the lines he will say, the plot that will unravel over the ensuing days. He knows what is to come but he still has to face the most dramatic days of his life. He still has to face an audience who will love him and hate him and hand him over to be tortured and executed. The time to act has dawned and the shadow of the cross falls across this stage of the life of Jesus.

A season of new life

Easter; that floating, movable feast. Easter; the weather could be warm and sunny, or filled with blustery winds and snowy showers. Easter; the celebration of the event that changed history. Easter; a story, not of a tiny baby and shepherds, wise men and angels, but of a man on a cross, a hideous death, an empty tomb, frightened disciples, timid as mice scurrying to their hiding holes who are transformed into lion-hearts. Easter; the promise of life beyond the grave. Easter; the cross of Christ, the forgiveness of God, the justice and mercy that met in perfect harmony and the world's darkest hour. The triumphal entry into the city riding on a donkey, the denial of Peter, the centurion who saw and said that this surely was a righteous man, the thief on the cross who asked Jesus to remember him when he came into his kingdom, the disciples at the empty tomb, the confounded soldiers and officials, the walk on the Emmaus road, the meeting on the shore, the brutality that Jesus suffered and the words he uttered from the cross. Easter. How can we take hold of such drama? How do we apply to our lives today the events that took place over two thousand years ago? How do we approach these ancient stories and allow them to impact our hearts and minds?

Whilst you are pondering these questions let me please ask you another. Do you like Easter eggs? I thought so. Yes, I know there are some of you who do not touch chocolate and the thought of gorging yourself silly on this substance leaves you in a cold sweat, but I think the majority of the population are with me in saying 'YES!'. I think there is something special in these chocolate eggs. Is it the wrapping? Or the packaging? Or just my imagination? Whatever the answer, the truth for me is that I love to devour chocolate Easter eggs. They taste delicious. There is a verse in the Bible, in the Psalms, that says 'Taste and see that the Lord is good'. In other words, we can experience for ourselves the reality of God in our lives. As we examine and explore the Easter story we shall find that it is not an academic treatise to be read in a passing, passive way. It is a story that we can engage heart and soul with, for it is a story where God gave his heart and soul for us.

A Father's heart

I can see the city,
almost hear the noise of the crowd,

the people
gathered inside her walls
and how,
how I wish that I could gather them,
draw them
to myself,
like a mother hen
protecting her chicks.
I would gather you under my wings,
provide shelter from the storms of life,
give peace to troubled minds,
if only
you would come to me –
not forced but freely –
then I could give you,
pour out to you,
my undying love.
For to you, my love,
I will pour out
my life;
for you, my beloved,
I will pour out
my life.

Bible reading

As he approached Jerusalem and saw the city, he wept over it and said, 'If you, even you, had only known on this day what would bring you peace – but now it is hidden from your eyes.'
Luke 19:41-42

Reflection

Have I hidden from God's love – or embraced his grace?
Have I tasted the goodness of God?

Prayer

Father God,
  thank you for your Son,
  who was prepared to make the journey to Jerusalem
  because of the joy that was set before him
  and that joy, as hard as it is to believe, was me.
Thank you with all my heart for your heart for me.
Amen.

Two

Transformations

It was hard to believe and yet totally believable. Lying in the safe, warm confines of the tent, I listened to the rain lashing against the canvas. It had been raining ever since I had woken up and, from the sound of the storm, it would be raining for a good while longer. I had no desire to crawl out of my sleeping bag. I simply wanted to curl up and go back to sleep. There was only one problem with my thinking, only one tiny flaw in my plan: we had to go home. As I lay in silence the rain seemed to be getting louder and louder. Was it just my imagination or was this the heaviest downpour of the century? It was only the summer of the year two thousand, I might hasten to add; early summer at that. There would be plenty more opportunities for torrential rain over the coming summer months!

Yesterday had been a glorious day; the sun had shone majestically and we had lapped it up. We started with a walk by the river in the tiny, picturesque village of Dent, nestled in the heart of the Yorkshire dales. After a picnic lunch by the water we had retired to the sports field and collapsed in the heat of the noonday sun (what was that saying about mad dogs and Englishmen?). The children continued to play and, now and again, I made some half-hearted attempt at kicking a football about, but that was the sum total of my exertions. It was way too hot to do anything except lay back and be thankful. A weekend break, a camping trip with our friends, the Lawsons – a lovely family who lived in our village – and we were delighted to be in sun-dappled Dent.

That was yesterday.

Today was the start of the monsoon weather. We decided to eat breakfast in a nearby café. The full English: bacon, eggs, the works. We knew that after we had eaten we would be taking down the tents in pouring rain and then driving home in damp, wet clothes. Oh, the joys of camping! Oh, what a transformation! One minute the sun is beating down and the next second rain water is running off the end of your nose. How quickly things change. Life can be like that. One moment everything is sunny and rosy, you and your family are well and healthy and then . . . disaster strikes! Out of the blue, without any warning, life is turned upside down and inside out. Illness, job loss, problems and the pressures of life come flooding in and you can strongly identify with the Beatles song 'Yesterday all my troubles seemed so far away'. Life can be like that. Life was like that for Jesus too. One minute he is riding into Jerusalem on a donkey to the adulation of the crowd. The people's favourite, everyone wants to meet him, to see him, and as the crowds gather so the praises pour out. Jesus was popular. He was loved and adored. He was worshipped. In weather terminology the sun was shining in a cloudless blue sky. It was heat wave time, without even a hint of a cloud on the horizon. What could possibly go wrong?

Everything.

The same crowd who were praising him were soon to be cursing him. The cheers were to turn to jeers and the love to hate. How fickle we can be, and how quickly a crowd can be turned. Soon there would be rain on the parade and the sky would turn to darkest black.

Soon . . .

But for now, for the moment, Jesus was honoured and welcomed as the people's saviour. How little did they understand what price the Saviour was going to have to pay.

Bible reading

When he came near the place where the road goes down the Mount of Olives, the whole crowd of disciples began joyfully to praise God in loud voices for all the miracles they had seen:

'Blessed is the king who comes in the name of the Lord!'

'Peace in heaven and glory in the highest!'

Some of the Pharisees in the crowd said to Jesus, 'Teacher, rebuke your disciples!'

'I tell you,' he replied, 'if they keep quiet, the stones will cry out.'

Luke 19:37-40

Stone me!

Characters:

Stone 1, Stone 2, Crowd (This sketch would work equally well without a crowd, just starting from the two stones talking)

Scene:

A crowd of people lined up by the roadside. Like a domino effect they lay down their cloaks. Having done this they wave their arms in the air then reach over to their opposite number in the line to form an arch, then freeze. On the other side of the stage are two people. No one knows they are stones.

(1 opens their mouth and puts their hands in the air as if they are going to shout out loud. 2 puts their hand over 1's mouth to prevent them from uttering a sound.)

2 What do you think you're playing at?

(1 makes a muffled sound. 2 releases their hand from 1's mouth.)

1 What do you think you are playing at?

2 Stopping you.

1 Why? What have I done wrong? What have I ever done wrong in my entire life?

2 Nothing.

1 So what's with the 'stick a pebble in my mouth' routine?

2 Because you were going to, you know . . .

1 No, I don't know that you know what I know what you think I know if you don't know enough to tell me what you think I know I know, you don't know.

(1 stares at 2 who stares back)

2 No good giving me that stony look.

1 And you're not?

2 I can't help the way I look.

1 But you can help the way you act.

2 But it was your actions that concern me.

1 My actions?

2 Yes, your actions.

1 My actions? Which ones are those then?

2 The ones you were going to do.

1 Oh, those actions. The actions you say you know but you don't know because if you did know then you would know that every-one knows . . .

2 SHUT UP!

1 No need to shout.

2 But that's exactly what you were going to do.

1 Yes, I . . . how did you know?

2 I know, OK. I just know. Ever since 'the arrival' you've been in a right state. You've been rolling all over the place.

1 Yeah, but I haven't gathered any moss.
(1 brushes themself down)

2 I'm not saying you have, I'm just saying you were very excited. But no matter how much boulder you feel, you can't shout out.

1 Even if I feel really bold?

2 No matter if you were the biggest boulder on the block. Ssh!!
(2 puts their finger on their lips)

1 But you heard His Majesty.

2 Of course I did. We all hear his voice.

1 'Even the stones would cry out and praise me', that's what His Majesty said.

2 Only if the people didn't.

1 Oh.

2 And what are the people doing?

1 Attacking one another with tree branches?

2 Sometimes you're such a brick. They're worshipping. They're passionate with their emotions, extravagant in their love. That's the way they were created. We, on the other hand . . .

1 If we had a hand.

2 . . . were made to reflect his glory in a different way. OK? So no acts of boldness, please.
(1 looks, opens their mouth, nothing; bows, then kneels)
Freeze.

Reflection

Do I keep quiet or speak up for Jesus?
Do I go along with the crowd or make a stand for what I believe in?

Prayer

Father God,
thank you for the humility of your Son who chose to ride on a donkey.
Thank you for all of those people who recognised Jesus as the Messiah, the Saviour.
Thank you that we can worship you and lay our lives before you today.
Amen.

Three

Of real value

Here is a confession: I am not a happy shopper. If I had to compile a top ten list of favourite pastimes then shopping would not feature anywhere on my chart. Over the years I have tried to take a mature view of shopping – it is necessary when you need to buy things like food, and I must say that I have made some improvement in this department. When my wife Claire was pregnant I took on sole responsibility for our weekly supermarket shop, and got the job down to such a fine art that I posted a 12-minute time on the clock, a record which stands to this day. Yes, I do like to get the shopping over and done with in double quick time, whereas Claire takes a rather different view. She likes to read the labels, check the ingredients, compare the prices. I just want her to sling things into the trolley so that we can whiz on to the next aisle. She continually wanders backwards and forwards, as if time stood still in her saunter around the supermarket.

I am not a happy shopper but I am learning, slowly.

There is, however, a time when shopping is pleasurable, a time when I can go as far as saying I really enjoy traipsing around the shops.

The January sales!

Bargain after bargain greets my eyes as I load up with goodies. Maybe it's the Yorkshireman in me, the Barnsley that you cannot take out of me, but I do love a bargain! What amazes me, and sometimes annoys me, is how the prices drop so astronomically. Now, this is great when I can stand in a shop with a smug smile on my face thinking, 'I am so glad that I didn't make that particular purchase just before Christmas' but (and there is always a but), I hate it, and feel down-right disgusted and cheated, when I see something that I have spent my last pennies on before Christmas only to see said item now at a rock bottom, we-will-pay-you-money-to-take-this-product-out-of-our-shop kind of price. Such a sight and such a feeling has been known to taint or even spoil my happy little shopping spree. I know I should look on things logically and philosophically – 'you win some and you lose some' – but, as I have stated, shopping does not bring out my finer qualities.

Sorry.

The thought does go through my mind, though: 'What real value is the item?' Is it the sale price – the super-slashed, knocked down, never-to-be-bettered-or-beaten price, or is it the shop price it started at? Which is it? Life can be full of changing values, and not just because of sales. As Jesus enters the city of Jerusalem he makes for the temple, and what does he do on arrival? He drives out all the traders. He is appalled at what the temple has become. In Jesus' own words the charge is made: 'My house will be a house of prayer, but you have made it a den of robbers.' The value had changed; as the money had changed hands, so the place had become not a house of prayer but a place for making profit. On witnessing this scene Jesus takes strong action. He drives them out. He doesn't politely ask them to leave but gets rid of them.

This is a part of the nature of God that we may sometimes struggle with: a God of fiery passion. It is a sign to me of how much God cares and, although he is patient and loving with us, he will not tolerate sin and hypocrisy. The words that he spoke to the church in Laodiciea spring to mind: 'I know your deeds, that you are neither cold nor hot. I wish you were either one or the other! So, because you are lukewarm – neither hot nor cold – I am about to spit you out of my mouth. You say, "I am rich; I have acquired wealth and do not need a thing." But you do not realise that you are wretched, pitiful, poor, blind and naked. I counsel you to buy from me gold refined in the fire, so that you can become rich; and white clothes to wear, so that you can cover your shameful nakedness; and salve to put on your eyes, so that you can see.

'Those whom I love I rebuke and discipline. So be earnest, and repent. Here I am! I stand at the door and knock. If anyone hears my voice and opens the door, I will come in and eat with him, and he with me.'

Revelation 3:15-20

Strong, powerful words. Words that warn and rebuke and yet words which flow from a Father's heart of love. The knock on the door. The handle which only we can open. Will we invite the Lord God into our lives or keep him on the outside? Will we fall in love with false religion or our own foolish ways, or will we fall in love with the God of love? It is far better to have our lives emptied of the wrong things, the upturned values, and be put right in our relationship with God. Far better to respond now whilst we have the opportunity.

But will we?

Not my kind of profit!

Scene: A man clearing up his stall. He is not very happy!

Man The man has no manners – none.

Just look at this mess *(he gestures with his arm)* and did he stop to help me pick it up? Not on your life! I thought he was supposed to be such a 'kind' man. *(Says this with sarcasm in his voice)* He doesn't care about my business, does he? And my business is none of his business.

What's it got to do with him? *(He is now starting to get really worked up)* Who does he think he is? Hmm? Storming in here, upturning the tables. Someone ought to turn the tables on him! *(Stops and thinks about what he has just said, a plan beginning to hatch in his mind)*

What kind of a prophet is he anyway? One who doesn't care about 'real' profit. Does the man have any sense of real values? I wonder what it will cost to get rid of him? One thing's for sure, it will be worth it. The man is a menace.

Next thing you know this place will be full of people praying again. Not that I have anything against prayer, you understand. Not when it is in its proper place and proper time. But not taking centre stage – come on, be real, we have businesses to run . . . and I have some business to take care of. *(He gives a look of intent and freezes)*

Reflection

What do I value most in my life?
What do I consider to be most profitable in my life?

Prayer

Father God, thank you that you are a God who cares passionately.
Please forgive my foolish ways and help me to live my life by the values of your kingdom.
Amen.

Four

The kiss of death

He is a fascinating character and a complex person. How do you begin to unravel the mystery that is Judas? Just the very mention of his name can cause a shiver or revulsion, or perhaps some confusion. How could one of the twelve, one of the closest followers of Jesus, betray him? How? Is there an answer to this mystery, to this enigma? What were his reasons, his motives? Was he propelled by pure profit? Was he trying to force some action, feeling frustrated that Jesus wasn't showing enough of his power and strength? Was it just destiny? Jesus would be crucified and the lot simply fell to Judas. What is the answer? In raising the questions I am not sure if I can deliver the verdict, but we can all examine the evidence.

Judas was a disciple of Jesus, for whatever reasons he chose to follow. He had witnessed with his own eyes the miracles, heard with his own ears the message but what had taken place in his own heart? Again, we cannot know for sure. All we can do is look at his actions. Jesus said that 'by your fruits you will be known'. The fruits that Judas displayed are there to be seen. His pocketing of the funds and his thinking regarding the anointing of Jesus are examples of Judas' character. In the end he acted – he took matters into his own hands and went to betray Jesus. Did he know what the outcome would be? Did he have any idea of the consequences that would lead to the crucifixion? Once more, we are not certain but what is in evidence is that Judas hung himself. For all of his actions and deeds he was eventually overcome by remorse. To know that Jesus was going to suffer, and that he had played a crucial part in the proceedings, was too much for him to bear. He killed himself.

Judas – the Judas kiss of betrayal.

A man whose actions led to the arrest and execution of Jesus.

A man who will forever be remembered as the disciple who not only deserted Jesus but actually betrayed him.

We wouldn't do such a thing like that, would we?

Bible reading

And Judas went to the chief priests and the officers of the temple guard and discussed with them how he might betray Jesus.
Luke 22:4

What if?

It is easy to look at others
and see their faults,
failures
and misdemeanours.
It is easy to see the speck of sawdust in someone else's eye
whilst ignoring the plank in our own.
It is easy to see the characters
in the Bible,
the chronicles of their catastrophes
and think
'I would never do that'.
But would we?

If we were there
in their shoes,
facing those pressures,
temptations,
obstacles
and hurdles –
how do we know,
how do we know?
It is easy to judge,
even when
we are told not to.
It is harder,
much harder,
to see our own faults,
to be honest
about our own life
and our own weaknesses
and failures,
but
there is a saying
that is worth repeating:
'there but for the grace of God go I.'
'There but for the grace,
the grace of God,
go I.'

Reflection

Do I look upon my own life with sober judgment or just judge others?
Do I show sympathy and understanding towards others and their situations?

Prayer

Father God, thank you that you are a God of grace and mercy.
Thank you that you always make the right judgments.
Help me not to judge others but to love them as you do.
Amen.

Five

Now do you understand?

World Cups and major sporting championships are full of them.

Tactics.

How is your team going to play? What about the opposition? What do you do if plan A proves a complete flop? Do you have a back-up plan? Does everyone know what that back-up plan is? How will you cope when the heat is on? Will you wilt under pressure or stand up to be counted? Have you listened to the coach's instructions? Do you trust your teammates to perform? Do you wish you were not about to perform in front of two billion people? (The estimated anticipated audience for the football World Cup final). Two billion people! Can you imagine playing and being watched by a third of the population of this planet? Can you imagine what kind of pressure you would feel? I don't think I'd even be able to tie up my football boots – mind you, I never can!

The pressure to perform. The right tactics to win.

As the disciples sat around a meal table, enjoying their food and each other's company, did they understand what Jesus was saying to them? Did they have any true understanding of what Jesus was going to go through for them? He wasn't like some kind of football coach who was going to give them all a good pep talk and send them out onto the pitch. Oh no, Jesus was the one who was going to step out into the arena. He was the one who was going to face the enemy. He was the one who was going to do battle.

Did they understand the game plan?

As they finished their meal and the wine sat on the table, and Jesus picked up the loaf of bread and began to speak, did they have ears to hear? Did they comprehend the depth of what Jesus was saying? He wasn't laying down the plans to win some world cup, he was sharing how he was going to win the greatest of battles: the defeat of death and sin.

Did they know how much it would cost him?

As the wine was drunk, and Jesus stared into the cup, I wonder what went through their minds?

I wonder what effect these words, spoken by Jesus, have on us today?

I wonder?

Bible reading

When the hour came, Jesus and his apostles reclined at the table. And he said to them, 'I have eagerly desired to eat this Passover with you before I suffer. For I tell you, I will not eat it again until it finds fulfilment in the Kingdom of God.'

After taking the cup, he gave thanks and said, 'Take this and divide it among you. For I tell you I will not drink again of the fruit of the vine until the kingdom of God comes.'

And he took bread, gave thanks and broke it, and gave it to them, saying, 'This is my body given for you; do this in remembrance of me.'

In the same way, after the supper he took the cup, saying, 'This cup is the new covenant in my blood, which is poured out for you.'
Luke 22:14-20

'Remember'

'In remembrance of me.'
'In remembrance of me.'
Break the bread,
   drink the wine.
'In remembrance of me.'
'In remembrance of me.'
A symbol,
   a sign
   of
   a Saviour
   who suffered
   and
   sacrificed.
'In remembrance of me.'
'In remembrance of me.'
Those soon-to-be
   nail-
   scarred hands
   break the bread,
   pour the wine.
'In remembrance of me.'
'In remembrance of me.'
The meal finishes,
   a city sleeps,
   whilst soldiers
   march
   upon a garden.
'In remembrance of me.'

'In remembrance of me.'
An arrest,
   an injustice
   against
   the Almighty,
   whose body
   breaks,
   whose blood
   pours.
'In remembrance of me.'
'In remembrance of me.'
A world weeps,
   the curtain tears,
   and
   the power of sin
   breaks,
   and
   death
   loses its sting.
'In remembrance of me.'
'In remembrance of me.'
Bread,
   wine,
   cross,
   tomb
   empty.
'Remember me.'

Reflection

What do I remember when I think of the symbols of the bread and the wine?
How do I feel about the communion?

Prayer

Father God, thank you for the simple signs and symbols that you gave us to help us remember, and never forget, the pain and the agony that you endured so that we might know you.
Amen.

Six

The test

It was a grey, dismal day in October. The kind of day when you wish you could just roll over, ignore the alarm and stay in bed, especially when you have . . . your driving test.

The weather was still grey and gloomy at the start of my test. It was rush hour in the town of Barnsley as I embarked on my journey. I didn't know where I was going but the instructor did. Sitting with his clip-board and pen he was ready for action!

It didn't take long before he began filling in his piece of paper. The moment I reversed the car around a street corner only to find that I had parked in the middle of the road, I heard the sound of a pen scrawling across paper. Well, I hadn't hit the curb, but I did nearly reach the other side of the road. Was all lost?

Maybe not then, but what about after my hill start? Or should I say, when I started rolling down the hill, getting faster and faster. The car had stalled as I had approached a junction and it began to descend down a steep slope. The car wasn't the only thing which had stalled. My brain wasn't in gear at all. What should I do? If only my brain was working then it might have been inclined to tell me.

The car continued to roll.

A thought that did flash through my mind was about the cars coming up the hill, probably wondering why my car was rapidly reversing towards them. If only I had the answer.

Thankfully, the instructor did.

He yanked on my handbrake and stared at me.

There were big sounds of pen touching paper, and I knew then that my test was over. Or should I say, I knew I had failed but unfortunately my test wasn't over. Oh no, not quite over yet.

Time was almost up and we were heading back to the test centre when I pulled over at the lights. I did all my correct checks: mirror, signal, manoeuvre, apply the brakes, put on the handbrake and calmly slip the car into neutral; as Del Boy from *Only Fools and Horses* would have said, 'Lovely jubbly'.

'Why have you stopped?' asked the examiner.

The tone of voice was a mixture of inquisitiveness and incredulity. I was about to say 'Because I'm at the traffic lights' when my eye caught the colour.

Green.

How long it had been at green I had no idea. I moved away quickly. I failed. No surprise there, no shock at all. In fact, I was mightily relieved that we had all survived.

A few months later I took my test again. Not that I want to be at all boastful but I was good. From being appallingly bad I was now driving with confidence and control. The examiner was polite and friendly as he asked me the questions at the end of my test. I obliged him with the answers and sat back waiting for the good news.

'You've failed.'

I couldn't believe it, nor could the wall believe it when I kicked it as I walked home. It was on a minor and, may I hasten to add, debatable point, but I had failed.In frustration my foot caught a stone wall. No complaints from the wall, thankfully, but my foot was killing me. So too were these tests. I couldn't keep going through this. I couldn't do it, but my wife said I could.

Third test: chief examiner, longest test, pen on paper for one 'iffy' manoeuvre. Questions that I couldn't answer because by the time we had returned to the centre I had given up all hope. The man just kept firing questions at me and I just wanted to go home.

The chief examiner looked at me. The ordeal was over.

'You've passed.'

I couldn't believe it!

The examiner's face never smiled – in fact, he gave me a few driving tips as I left the vehicle – but I had passed.

All of these years later the memories are not only etched into my memory, they are coloured in. I had been so close to giving up, I nearly had, but, with the help, support and encouragement of my wife, I had carried on. We didn't have a car, and wouldn't for a while, but little did I know then how crucial driving for me would be when I became a schools' worker.

Failure is a part of life – at least, it is in mine! I am sure that we have all failed in some things, some more serious than others. The big question is: do we give in? Do we give up when the going gets tough? Do we walk away or do we keep on going? As we look at the dramatic events of that first Easter we are faced with the abject failure of Peter. The disciple who had dared to speak out and declare his allegiance to Jesus. No matter if others were to fail Jesus, he never would, or so he thought. Or so he thought . . .

Bible reading

Then seizing him, they led him away and took him into the house of the high priest. Peter followed at a distance. But when they had kindled a fire in the middle of the courtyard and had sat down together, Peter sat down with them. A servant girl saw him seated there in the firelight. She looked closely at him and said, 'This man was with him.'

But he denied it. 'Woman, I don't know him,' he said.

A little later someone else saw him and said, 'You also are one of them.'

'Man, I am not!' Peter replied.

About an hour later another asserted, 'Certainly this fellow was with him, for he is a Galilean.'

Peter replied, 'Man, I don't know what you're talking about!' Just as he was speaking, the cock crowed. The Lord turned and looked straight at Peter. Then Peter remembered the word the Lord had spoken to him: 'Before the cock crows today, you will disown me three times.'

And he went outside and wept bitterly.

Luke 22:54-62

A penitent prayer

I never knew him.
I never knew him.
I never knew him.
How could I . . . ?
I can't believe . . .
I knew him.
I knew his call on my life,
  knew his kindness and compassion,
  knew his grace and his goodness.
I knew him,
  knew his love for the lost,
  knew his friendship in my life.
I knew him.

So how could I, betray,
  deny,
  turn away
  from him,
  from him?
How could I?
What must he have thought? felt?
  when he heard,
  when he saw,
  when his eyes met mine;
  his eyes met mine.
What must he think of me now?
I knew him
  but
  I didn't know how to stand up for him,
  didn't know how to speak up for him,
  didn't know how to simply be there for him.
I knew him
  but now he knows
  my failure,
  my fears,
  my folly.
Will he want to know me,
  will he want know me
  will he want to know
  me?

Reflection

Do I know the mercy and grace of God in my life?
Do I realise that failing doesn't mean that I'm finished?

Prayer

Father God,
thank you for forgiveness.
Thank you for restoration and renewal when we fail you, fail others, fail ourselves.
Thank you that there is a way back, there is hope and there is peace to receive from you.
Thank you for Peter's story, for its honesty and hope for all of us who know what it is like to deny you in our lives and let you down.
Thank you that the story doesn't end there, and neither does it have to be the finish for us too.
Thank you that, knowing us better than we know ourselves, you love us completely.
Amen.

Seven

Break out

As we strolled back by the river I reflected on what had been a beautiful day. It wasn't just beautiful because the sun had shone and an early April day had been filled with warm, sunny rays. It had been beautiful because we had enjoyed a wonderful fifth birthday for our son Joseph. Now, after watching the film *Ice Age* in Kendal, we had just finished our fish and chips sitting by the river. Idyllic in every way. The walk back to the car was gentle and relaxed. A perfect day. What could possibly go wrong?

The barrier.

The barrier of the car park was down.

I decided not to panic but it was too late – I was already panicking. The barrier was down and the gates were locked. Our car was sat on the top floor of the multi-storey. The sign, which I had obviously not read earlier, told me we had just missed 'lock up'. All entrances were locked. There was not a soul in sight. The day was rapidly cooling and Joseph looked like he was about to start shivering. We were low on cash and lived miles away.

Help!

'I think I need to phone Pete and Jill,' I informed Claire.

She readily agreed.

Having family living in the next village to us was a joy in many ways. One of them was that you always felt you could ask your family to come and rescue you when you were stranded and your car was locked up for the night.

I ran to find a phone.

My conversation was short and loaded: 'Pete, are you doing anything tonight?'

He said he would come and collect us.

I walked back to Claire and Joseph with some sense of relief.

They were not there. Neither was my sense of relief.

I hadn't a clue where they could have gone or why they would go anywhere else. I told myself not to panic but the order had come through too late again. I already was panicking.

Running up and down the shopping precinct I saw Claire talking to a strange man. Not that the man was 'strange', just that we didn't know him.

'I was just praying,' said Claire, 'when this man appeared inside the shops. He opened the door and said he would go and turn all the alarms off and remove the barrier.'

Great news!

I had just asked Pete to come and fetch us.

I have never run as fast in my life. Racing back to the phone booth I punched the digits and waited for a response.

It was Jill speaking.

'Has Pete gone?' came my wheezy, breathless voice.

'He's just on . . .'

'Stop him!'

Pete was stopped.

I now had to make the same sprint back to the car park where the man was about to unlock the barrier.

Made it!

All's well that ends well. It looked like there was no hope until a man with some keys materialised and made it possible for the barrier to be removed. What a relief.

Maybe we have all had similar experiences, not with car parks, but with situations in life. We thought we had blown it, lost it, thought we were in for it, our last chance saloon about to close, when all of a sudden, out of the blue, the cavalry appear on the horizon. The rescue, the help, the 'cavalry', may take different shapes or forms but we are mightily relieved to see them. What once seemed hopeless, what once seemed a lost cause, has now been reversed.

I wonder how this character in the Bible felt when his hopeless situation was reversed?

Breakout

Scene: A man comes running onto stage. He is overwhelmed with emotion and absolutely ecstatic.

Man Yes! Yes! Yes! *(He punches the air with his fists and even leaps into the air)*

Thank you, thank you for voting for me, thank you so much.

Thank you. *(He drops to his knees, overcome, relieved, grateful but then he pauses, stops to think and his mood changes)*

But why?

Why did you vote for me?

You don't even know me? You never came and visited me. Never brought me food to eat. Never once did I see any of your faces.

So why? Why did you do it? *(He is now back on his feet and looking hard at everyone trying to make sense out of what's just happened)*

When I was there in my cell I could hear the guards talking, whispering to one another, going on about this man, this Jesus. One of the soldiers told a story about him, how he had seen him when he had entered the city. The crowds, full of praises, proclaimed him to be the Messiah, the Saviour. The Saviour?

Who would want to crucify the Saviour?

Why me? *(He pauses, looks around, looks over his shoulder, thinks about the cross)*

It should have been me. I should be the one on the hill, carrying my cross, crucified for my crimes. It should have been me. *(He slowly sits down, slumped on the ground. He casts a look once again at the crosses on the hill.)*

It should have been me.

Bible reading

With one voice they cried out, 'Away with this man! Release Barabbas to us!'

(Barabbas had been thrown into prison for an insurrection in the city, and for murder.)

Wanting to release Jesus, Pilate appealed to them again. But they kept shouting 'Crucify him! Crucify him!'

For the third time he spoke to them: 'Why? What crime has this man committed? I have found in him no grounds for the death penalty. Therefore I will have him punished and then release him.'

But with loud shouts they insistently demanded that he be crucified, and their shouts prevailed. So Pilate decided to grant their demand. He released the man who had been thrown into prison for insurrection and murder, the one they asked for, and surrendered Jesus to their will. Luke 23:18-25

Reflection

How do you feel about the guilty going free?
How do you think Barabbas might have felt?

Prayer

Father God,
thank you for your son, Jesus.
Thank you that he was willing to become the guilty one so that we can go free.
Thank you for removing the barrier of sin, something we couldn't possibly have done.
Amen.

Eight

All for love

'Have you ever hugged a tree?'

I looked at my wife but was quite speechless.

'Have you hugged a tree?'

I didn't know how to respond or where to begin. Should I say, 'No of course I haven't hugged a tree. Are you mad, woman?', or perhaps laugh and joke it off: 'You've hugged a tree, I hug them all the time, on my way to work, on my weekends. Show me a tree and I'll give it a hug.'

I said nothing.

'Have you hugged a tree?'

I knew that my stalling tactics were running out of time.

'No,' came my calm, casual response, 'I have not hugged a tree.'

'Never?'

'Never.'

'Don't you want to?'

'No,' came my very hasty reply.

'Not even for me?'

'No.'

My wife looked at me, studying my face.

'What about that tree? It's a lovely tree.'

Now let me set the record straight here. I like trees; I love trees. They are wonderful to look at, very aesthetically pleasing to the eye. But I have no desire to touch.

'Please, for me?' said my wife, with her big eyes looking straight into mine.

'No.'

'Go on, please, for me, just once?'

'How can I say this? No.'

Claire was gazing at the trees in the woods.

'Please?'

'No.'

'I've hugged trees.'

'I won't tell anyone.'

'It's good.'

'U-huh.'

'Please, just once, for me, if you love me?'

Oh why, oh why, those words and why, oh why, those eyes, that voice, that look? Why? I stood in the middle of the woods with my wife surrounded by trees and I had to pick one to hug.

'If you love me,' she said.

I hugged a tree.

'It's good, isn't it?' asked my wife.

'I am not doing it again, ever.' And that was the end of the conversation. It is amazing what things you will do for someone you love. What silly things you may say, what extremes you may go to. You can look back at some of your antics and smile, laugh or cringe with embarrassment, but the truth is love makes us do things we never, ever, thought we would. Ask a certain tree and it will tell you!

There is another tree that knows a story, a powerful story about love: the tree that Jesus was nailed to. He didn't wrap his arms around it but allowed his hands and feet to be nailed to it. He allowed himself to be put on a piece of wood because of love. Because of his undying love for each one of us, Jesus died.

Two thousand years

Tortured,
Whipped,
Oppressed.

Then
Hanged,
Our
Undesired
Saviour;
And
Now
Death.

Yet
Eternal
And
Risen
Son.

Bible reading

When they came to the place called the Skull, there they crucified him, along with the criminals – one on his right, the other on his left. Jesus said, 'Father, forgive them, for they do not know what they are doing.'
Luke 23:33-34a

Reflection

How do you feel about God's love for you?
How do you feel about the cross?

Prayer

Father God,
thank you for the cross.
What can I say?
What words can convey my gratitude, my thanks, my love for you?
You died for me.
You, who were so innocent, took my wrongs upon your shoulders and bled for me.
What amazing love, that the Creator should carry the cross for the created, and that God should give his life for me.
Father,
I stand humbled and in awe at the foot of the tree on which you died for me.
Amen.

Nine

Now do you understand?

'Pick him up, quick.'

I dashed over to our son and scooped him up. Claire put her finger inside his mouth and fished around.

'Have you got it?'

Claire's concentrated face returned my question.

'Got it!'

Claire held up the piece of soggy Christmas wrapping paper. We gave a collective sigh of relief. Joseph didn't look at all perturbed and was busily eyeing up the rest of the wrapping.

Christmas Day. Our son's first Christmas and we had bought him a wonderful hand-made fire engine. It had been beautifully wrapped by my wife and I had been allocated the job of cameraman to capture these precious moments. I had filmed whilst Claire helped Joseph with all the wrapping paper, and then zoomed in as he was face to face with his present, his brand-new gift. Claire had retreated from the scene so she could watch and enjoy too. The next thing that I saw through my lens was Joseph eating the wrapping paper! He wasn't at all interested in the gift, just the wrapping. Hopefully he will learn!

How about us? And I am not talking about understanding that we don't eat Christmas paper. I sincerely hope that we all know that! But there is another gift given that we need to grasp the meaning of:

'For the wages of sin is death, but the gift of God is eternal life in Christ Jesus our Lord.'
Romans 6:23.

The wage that we deserve is 'death' and that wage is something that we have all earned.

'For all have sinned and fall short of the glory of God.'
Romans 3:23.

Not one of us is good enough to reach God's standards. That is the bad news, but the good news is that no one is excluded from receiving the gift.

No one.

Too late?

Dear Mum,
I guess you're surprised to hear from me?
  Me too.
I'm sorry for . . .
  you know.
Mum,
  I'm scared and I don't know what to say; I don't have long now.
Mum,
  I know I should have, could have, done better.
  I know if Dad had been alive things,
  well, life would have been better.
I hope you can forgive me,
  I hope you will be all right.
Mum,
  I'm going be crucified because I'm a criminal.
  The other guy in my cell is just cursing,

blaming everyone but himself.
I know I've done wrong,
it's just that saying sorry
doesn't seem good enough.
Mum,
I hope you get this letter,
and see that, even though it's too late,
I am truly sorry.
Mum,
I have to go,
I love you.

Bible reading

One of the criminals who hung there hurled insults at him: 'Aren't you the Christ? Save yourself and us!'

But the other criminal rebuked him. 'Don't you fear God,' he said, 'since you are under the same sentence? We are punished justly, for we are getting what our deeds deserve. But this man has done nothing wrong.'

Then he said, 'Jesus, remember me when you come into your kingdom.'

Jesus answered him, 'I tell you the truth, today you will be with me in paradise.'
Luke 23:39-43

We don't know the conversation that the thieves might have had shortly before their crucifixion but we do know what they said to Jesus on the cross. One of them reviled Jesus and one of them reached out to him. One of them rejected paradise and one of them received.

Reflection

Which one of the criminals are you?
How do you feel about Jesus' response to the criminal?

Prayer

Father God,
thank you for your gift of eternal life.
Thank you that, although I can never earn it, I can receive it.
Amen.

Ten

Can you tell what it is yet?

Rolf Harris

Now famous for his presenting of the programme *Animal Hospital*, Rolf is a very multi-talented man who has been around in the arena of show business for a long time. A singer, comedian, and artist. During one of his earlier programmes he had a slot in the show where he would do painting. The whole piece was a real work of art; not just the final product but the way in which he would talk his way through the creative process. Right up until the final brushstroke you couldn't really tell what it was. Rolf would paint with big brush strokes, and often vivid colours splashed across the canvas. During the painting he would stop and say 'Can you tell what it is yet?' – a wonderful catch phrase uttered in his Australian drawl. From being totally clueless to the clarity of the finished picture, it was fun to watch. Amidst a wild assortment of shapes and colours, the whole scene would suddenly make sense, and an acknowledging smile and nod was given when the final stroke had been completed. 'Now I see what it is, now I see.'

Life can be full of situations that are like that. We hear snippets of conversations but don't really know what the conversation is about. We hear one side of an argument but not the other. We see life through our own experiences and prejudices. We make snap judgments without finding out all the facts. Life can be like that.

In one of the final scenes at the foot of the cross we are drawn into the dialogue of the Centurion, the Roman soldier who presumably was on duty when Jesus was being crucified. His words are recorded in the Gospel account. When you consider who this person was – a member of a conquering army, a hardened and seasoned soldier – then it is extremely poignant what he says. Had he heard Jesus speak? Did he know much about him? The narrative doesn't tell us but, right at the end of Jesus' life, the Centurion makes an exclamation that reveals he finally sees who Jesus really is.

Bible reading

It was now about the sixth hour, and darkness came over the whole land until the ninth hour, for the sun stopped shining. And the curtain of the temple was torn in two. Jesus called out with a loud voice, 'Father, into your hands I commit my spirit.' When he had said this, he breathed his last.

The centurion, seeing what had happened, praised God and said, 'Surely this was a righteous man.'
Luke 23:44-47

The centurion speaks

I'm just a soldier,
doing my duty,
doing my duty.
Please understand,
I didn't want to,
it wasn't . . .

I was just doing my duty,
walking up the hill.
I tried to help him,
saw him crash to the ground,
the weight of the cross
crushing his body
as he lay on the floor.
I pulled a man from the crowd,
ordered him,
commanded him
to carry his cross.
I saw his face,
his eyes look into mine,
as I lifted up his cross.
That body,
beaten,
bloody,
bruised,
beyond
recognition
from the man who had ridden triumphant
into the city.
And how could the crowds turn
from praises
to curses?
How could I be supervising
his execution?
But I was.
I was the one who was on duty,
who gave the command

that began
the hammering,
the knocking
of nails
into his hands,
his feet.
I was the one
who saw
his face,
who heard
his words.
I have seen dying men
ask for mercy,
but I have never seen a dying man
granting mercy:
'Father, forgive them',
that's what he said.
Forgive,
forgive,
forgive.
I have never seen a man like this before,
never seen a death like this before,
never heard words like his before.
'Surely
this was a righteous man',
I said.
But was he?
Was he just a man?

Reflection

Have you had only information about who Jesus is, or a revelation?
What do you think might have happened to the Centurion's own faith in Jesus?

Prayer

Father God,
thank you for the centurion who saw who Jesus was.
Please help me to know that same reality in my own life and to reveal Jesus to people who see my life.
Amen.

Eleven

Mummy's boy

You may have heard that phrase,'Mummy's boy'. It is often spoken in a not-so-flattering way: 'Oh, you're just a Mummy's boy!', often referring to someone who has been loved and looked after in such a way that they are quite soft and helpless, incapable of doing much because Mummy has always done it for them. Calling someone names is never a good thing anyway, but trying to rile someone because their mother has really cared and looked after them is very cruel. Maybe, in some cases, Mum has done more than was required and her son does need to learn a few things, but I believe the heart of a mother is to love her child. I can say that from personal experience because I have a wonderful mum who has shown her love to me in countless ways, and because I see in my wife another wonderful mum who has showered her love on our son. I know another mother who gave everything for her son: Mary. Jesus loved his mother too. The Gospel of John contains a very moving account of what Jesus says to his mum even while he is hanging on the cross.

'Near the cross of Jesus stood his mother, his mother's sister, Mary the wife of Clopas, and Mary Magdalene. When Jesus saw his mother there, and the disciple whom he loved standing near by, he said to his mother, "Dear woman, here is your son," and to the disciple, "Here is your mother." From that time on, this disciple took her into his home.
John 19:25-27

I can hardly begin to imagine the turmoil and the hurt that Mary would have been feeling. I know what we as parents experienced when our son had to have an operation and we knew that the surgeon's knife was going to have to cut into him, but for Mary . . . ?

To see her son on the cross, whom she had cradled as a babe in her arms, whom she had watched take his first steps – to now see spikes driven into his feet; hands, that she would have held as he took his first faltering steps, now nailed to a cross of wood.

Jesus, her son, in his last moments, spoke about her welfare. He cared for her right to the end, the mother he loved so much and the mother who loved him and had to suffer the unspeakable tragedy of watching her beloved son die.

Bible reading

But all those who knew him, including the women who had followed him from Galilee, stood at a distance, watching these things.
Luke 23:49

A mother's love

I am not a mother!
This may be stating the obvious
  but
  it is worth mentioning
  because
  I will never know
  the joy of carrying a child,
  what it's like
  to be kicked,

not by a six foot two defender
but by tiny feet
on the inside.
Nor will I experience
the pain
of childbirth,
but can take my wife's word that
'It hurt!'
I will not know that special bond
or feeling
that must exist
between the mother
and her child –
A love that sacrifices,
gives generously
from a well
so deep,
so full –
a mother's love.
So how can I understand
or know
the pain
and the hurt,
the agony
of the heart,
when a mother
loses her son,
when she actually sees
her baby
bloody

and bruised,
beaten
and scarred,
broken
and nailed
to a cross
made of wood?
How can I understand?

Reflection

How do we show our love and support to those who have been through, and currently are, suffering?
How do you feel about the love Jesus showed to his mother?

Prayer

Father God,
thank you that you really do understand everything that we go through,
that you really do know us better than we know ourselves,
and you care, care for each and everyone of us in all that we go through on our journey of life.
Amen.

Twelve

Against the odds

'Truth is stranger than fiction.'

That is the saying and I believe it to be true. I have read, and I have watched, stories that have been amazing and incredible, but they often pale in comparison with real life. We have probably all experienced similar situations. An article in a newspaper, a report on the news, an autobiography that we have read – real life astounds and astonishes us. I was reading only the other day (I forget the exact details) about a baby who had survived for days in the wreckage of an earthquake. This kind of amazing story isn't isolated either; there are other people who, against all the odds, have survived the most seemingly impossible situations. Even when life seems to be over and there is no way out, an exit sign appears and a miracle is born.

Not for Jesus.

Or so Joseph of Arimathea might have thought.

Jesus was dead.

How did Joseph know? He had collected Jesus' body for burial.

Bible reading

Now there was a man named Joseph, a member of the Council, a good and upright man, who had not consented to their decision and action. He came from the Judean town of Arimathea and he was waiting for

the kingdom of God. Going to Pilate, he asked for Jesus' body. Then he took it down, wrapped it in linen cloth and placed it in a tomb cut in the rock, one in which no-one had yet been laid. It was Preparation Day, and the Sabbath was about to begin.
Luke 23:50-54

Joseph was a man who had stood against the decision of the Council. Against the odds, he had not been prepared to go with the crowd. Yet his actions had not saved Jesus. Now he was going to look after the body and give him his family tomb as his resting place.

Or so he thought . . .

Joseph and Nicodemus

Scene: Two men walk silently across stage. Their heads are bowed, their bodies slumped. They walk on. Joseph sits on the floor, Nicodemus prefers to stand. Mary is already sitting there.

Joseph Do you want to talk?

Mary shakes her head.

Joseph I need to talk.

Nicodemus It's a free world.

Joseph I just don't know what to say.

Nicodemus What can you say?

Joseph I don't know.

Nicodemus How can anyone say anything? How can anyone make any sense of this?

He gestures behind him. Joseph holds his head in his hands and rubs his eyes.

Joseph I wish I'd spoken up.

Nicodemus Would it have made any difference?

Joseph I don't know.

Nicodemus says very quietly:

Nicodemus No one spoke up.

Joseph I could have tried. I could have said something, done something.

Nicodemus What?

Joseph I don't know.

Joseph stands up at this point. He is angry with what has happened and with himself.

Nicodemus Overturned the decision?

Joseph No.

Nicodemus Out-shouted the crowd?

Joseph No.

Nicodemus Over-run the soldiers?

Joseph No.

Nicodemus So what could you have done?

Joseph I could have been there for him. Done something. Said something. Showed him that . . .

Nicodemus Showed him what?

There is a pause.

Joseph That I cared.

Nicodemus I know.

Joseph But did he know?

Another pause.

Mary He knows.

Mary stands up and puts a hand on Joseph's arm. Both men look away into the distance.

Nicodemus He seemed to know everything, have all the answers and the questions. He set my mind puzzling for weeks: 'You must be born again.'

Nicodemus smiles at the recollection.

Joseph I feel like I only understood him when it was too late.

Nicodemus I know.

Mary I think I always understood *(she smiles)*. There are some things I've known, things I've treasured all my life.

She smiles at the memories, then wipes a tear away.

Joseph I thought the people knew him too. His entry into Jerusalem. The reaction of the crowds, the praises, the adoration, the worship. I thought, I really thought this was it, the Messiah. I dared to believe in him. I thought I saw something in him that was different.

Mary You did.

The two men look at each other.

Joseph So why?

Nicodemus tries to answer but cannot find the words.

Nicodemus I don't know, Joseph, I just don't know.

Pause.

Joseph Did you see his face, when he was on the cross?

Nicodemus Yes.

Joseph Even though he was bruised, beaten, bloody, there was something about his face. Do you know what I mean?

Mary There was love. Always love.

Joseph There was a peace too. Not just an acceptance of death, but something else behind those eyes.

Nicodemus I saw his eyes.

There is a pause.

Joseph 'Forgive them,' he said.

Nicodemus How could he?

Joseph I don't know.

Nicodemus But he said it.

Joseph And meant it.

Nicodemus I know. I know.

Joseph Did you stay to the end?

Nicodemus Yes.

Joseph Did you hear his final words?

Nicodemus Yes.

A pause.

Joseph 'It is finished.'

Nicodemus Then he bowed his head.

Joseph 'It is finished.' Words to say it was over, the race run, his life ending.

Nicodemus Is that how you saw it?

Joseph How else can you see it? We just buried him.

Nicodemus I know. I know. But there was something in his eyes, in his voice.

Joseph What?

Nicodemus	I don't know. Maybe it's just me, the day, everything. Oh, I don't know.
Joseph	No, go on. How did you see it? What did you hear?
	Pause.
Nicodemus	A beginning.
	Mary stands and smiles. She is tired and weary but carries a treasured hope in her heart.
Mary	Come on, it's late. I'm going home now. I need to rest, I need to be up early in the morning.
	Freeze.

(taken from *The Word that Changed the World*, Kevin Mayhew, 2001)

Reflection

Am I prepared to stand up against the crowd and against all the odds?

Do I realise the hope that we have in Jesus is against all the odds?

Prayer

Father God,
thank you for the example and inspiration of people like Joseph, people who are prepared to do what is right no matter what others think, say or do.
Please help me to have the same characteristics and integrity, I pray.
Amen.

Thirteen

Expectations and exclamations

It was early.

The walk to the jetty was a short but exhilarating one, despite the fact that I'd had no more than two hours sleep.

I followed the procession of torches, heard the sounds from the jungle and saw the palm trees swaying under the pale moonlight. I felt like pinching myself just to make sure this wasn't a dream. I resisted the urge. It was no dream; as strange and as surreal as it was, this experience was for real.

We stepped into the boat.

On the jetty was a small crowd of people who had come to wave us off. I looked at their faces, saw the huge smiles they were wearing, and beamed back. On the boat our friends were shivering. Pete and I laughed. For the first time in over a week I felt pleasantly cool.

The engine roared into life and water sprayed onto the wooden platform as we headed back down the river. I cast a wistful look at the village and the people waving to us as we sped away. Even though I could see it before my eyes I could scarce believe what had happened in my life. A phone call from my pastor in January, an invitation to a trip to Borneo, the provision of funds, the time off work, and an incredible few days spent in a remote jungle village without electricity, accessible only by river, that was hungry for the Gospel of Jesus. We had baptised people in the river, burned witchcraft charms, prayed with people and shared our faith. To say that I had never experienced anything like this before would be one of the greatest of understatements.

As the boat headed back to the city of Kuching I watched the big saucer-shaped moon sink in the sky and slide out of view over the silhouette of the city.

'Happy birthday,' I said to Pete.

He was 21 today.

My trip to Borneo was one of the most incredible experiences of my life and I don't have room here to write it all down (that's another book!). One of the things I learnt as a young Christian was that God was far bigger than I could imagine, that he was a God of the unexpected and a God of surprises, a God who could, and does, do amazing things. These are lessons I have had to keep on relearning, principles I have seen in practice on numerous occasions, sometimes in my very darkest moments . . .

It was early.

Dawn breaking, birds stirring, a chorus of feathered voices filling the air. Light ushering away the dark. The sun replacing the night watchman, ready for another day's duty. A world waking up, a new beginning, filled with promise and opportunities, filled with possibilities and rich potential.

A group of women journeying.

Dawn had broken but what would they feel about another new day when their hearts were broken?

Possibilities?

Promise?

Potential?

They were carrying spices to a tomb.

These women had a solemn mission, a duty to perform, a body to serve even though that body was dead and buried.

As they trudged along the path did they fall into conversation with one another or just keep in step? Did they open up their hearts or was the pain too raw to be revealed? Did they lean on each other for comfort or look into each others eyes? Did they have any idea of what they were going to find when they arrived?

Bible reading

On the first day of the week, very early in the morning, the women took the spices they had prepared and went to the tomb. They found the stone rolled away from the tomb, but when they entered, they did not find the body of the Lord Jesus. While they were wondering about this, suddenly two men in clothes that gleamed like lightning stood beside them. In their fright the women bowed down with their faces to the ground, but the men said to them, 'Why do you look for the living among the dead? He is not here; he has risen! Remember how he told you, while he was still with you in Galilee: "The Son of Man must be delivered into the hands of sinful men, be crucified and on the third day be raised again."' Then they remembered his words.

When they came back from the tomb, they told all these things to the Eleven and to all the others. It was Mary Magdalene, Joanna, Mary the mother of James, and the others with them who told this to the apostles. But they did not believe the women, because their words seemed to them like nonsense. Peter, however, got up and ran to the tomb. Bending over, he saw the strips of linen lying by themselves, and he went away, wondering to himself what had happened.
Luke 24:1-12

The first day

A tomb
    full of doubts.
A body
    full of evidence.
A stone
    around their heart.
A vision
    of glorious light.
A dawning
    of truth.
A resurrection
    of hope.
A glimpse
    of eternity.
A message
    of certainty.
A response
    of incredulity.
A desire
    of reality.
A race
    of expectancy.
A question
    of rationality.
A tomb,
    empty.
A hope
    rising.

A saviour
  walking,
  smelling the roses
  in the garden,
  filled
  with new life.

Reflection

Do I expect the unexpected from God?
Do I run to tell others that Jesus is risen?

Prayer

Father God,
  thank you for the miracle and the message posted at an empty tomb.
Amen.

Fourteen

Now do you see?

I was eleven. I was on a school holiday. I was hating every minute of it.

Sorry, maybe that is a slight exaggeration, but you get the picture. I was not a happy bunny.

My first time away from home, my big trip with my mates, ended up being a miserable week camping in the Lakes, made to go on route marches for some unspecified reason (probably the 'it'll do you good' philosophy). Sleepless nights, slogging days spent up mountains, spam for tea and insects to share my sleeping bag. I know I should have got over it by now but I was young and I had been led to believe that I was going to have fun! I think the worst moment for me was when we scaled Helvellyn. I use the word 'scaled' because I did a lot of scrambling about on my hands and knees near the summit.

Now there is an interesting word.

Summit; the peak of the mountain, the view from the top, the climactic achievement of all of our hard graft.

'It'll be worth it when you get to the top,' said the teacher, as he watched me huffing and puffing, carrying a rucksack the size of a department store.

'It'll be worth it,' promised the teacher, as he saw me collapse and lie exhausted at the back of the group.

'It'll be worth it,' he intoned, as he urged me, step by step, up the mountainside.

The view from the top.

The scenic sight.

The misty-eyed look, and it wasn't because I was overcome with emotion!

You couldn't see a thing, not a thing.

'Time to go back down,' said the teacher.

Yes!

The day was bright and sunny. The years had rolled by and now, after a few decades had passed, I was ready to go back up Helvellyn (it takes me a long time to get over things). We had a beautiful walk, my wife and I, on a lovely summer's day.

Clouds.

Mist.

Observing nothing.

'Time to go back down,' said Claire to me.

I concurred.

Would I ever see the view?

Another summer and another attempt. I had recovered much quicker this time from my disappointment and, with the encouragement of my brother-in-law, Pete, and his son Joshua, we were on our way again.

A lovely day. Pete carried his young son in a back pack. I did the 'right thing' and offered to share the load with Pete and carry Joshua. He declined the offer – it was a father-and-son thing. I was so glad that it was!

The summit.

The view.

The mists!

I slumped by the stone obelisks at the top and unwrapped my

cheese sandwiches. They tasted great – food always does when you're freezing cold, stuck at the top of a mountain.

'Time to go back down,' said Pete.

I agreed, wholeheartedly.

We began our descent but before we had taken more than a few steps something happened. The mists cleared. So quickly and swiftly did they lift, it was like watching somebody drawing back the curtains, and there was the panoramic view. I gasped. I gawped. I grabbed my camera. This was a moment to treasure and to savour.

By the time we had taken our snapshots of the scene the swirling clouds had rolled back again and it was all wrapped up once more, but . . . but I had seen the view. Just for a short while it had been revealed. The mountains and the scenery had been there all along, it had just been hidden from my eyes! Now why does that sound familiar?

Two men on their journey were also in a fog. They too were unable to see, only this time it wasn't a mountain top experience but a road to Emmaus. They were joined on their sorrowful walk by a stranger. This person listened to their conversation as they explained to him what had been going on in Jerusalem over the last few days. The stranger spoke next and piece by piece he began to unravel the whole history of the nation and eventually reveal the mystery of who he was.

It was obvious really

Scene: A man reading the Bible, he is looking very thoughtful and wise, nodding now and again and uttering words like, 'ah!', 'yes', 'um'.

Man It's obvious really, when you look at it. It's all there, you see, written down in black and white, as plain as the nose on your face, as clear as a moonlit night, as transparent as . . . as . . . a transparent thing that is very transparent. Of course, my friend struggled with it all but then, between you and me, he always does struggle. He means well, he's a good enough chap and all that but not always quick on the uptake, if you know what I mean, and I am sure that 'you' do see what I mean. Yes, yes, yes, it was all so simple really. I had a sneaky suspicion all along, actually. You see, he had that voice. I couldn't quite place it but I did so recognise it. I mean, I was glued to his every word, and wouldn't you be! Then there was his knowledge, well that really ought to have given the game away. Oh, I know I asked him a few little questions about where he had been and didn't he know what had been going on in Jerusalem, but that was just to . . . just to, er, get things going, you see, you do see don't you? Good, good, I knew you would understand. I understand perfectly myself now, now that I've met him. Jesus, risen from the tomb. He came to my house for tea, you know. *(He says this with a big smile on his face. Freezes.)*

Bible reading

Now that same day two of them were going to a village called Emmaus, about seven miles from Jerusalem. They were talking with each other about everything that had happened. As they talked and discussed these things with each other, Jesus himself came up and walked along with them; but they were kept from recognising him.

He asked them, 'What are you discussing together as you walk along?'

They stood still, their faces downcast. One of them, named Cleopas, asked him, 'Are you only a visitor to Jerusalem and do not know the things that have happened there in these days?'

'What things?' he asked.

'About Jesus of Nazareth,' they replied. 'He was a prophet, powerful in word and deed before God and all the people. The chief priests and our rulers handed him over to be sentenced to death, and they crucified him; but we had hoped that he was the one who was going to redeem Israel. And what is more, it is the third day since all of this took place. In addition, some of our women amazed us. They went to the tomb early this morning but didn't find his body. They came and told us that they had seen visions of angels, who said he was alive. Then some of our companions went to the tomb and found it just as the women had said, but him they did not see.'

He said to them, 'How foolish you are, and how slow of heart to believe all that the prophets have spoken! Did not the Christ have to suffer these things and then enter his glory?' And beginning with Moses and all the Prophets, he explained to them what was said in all the Scriptures concerning himself.

As they approached the village to which they were going, Jesus acted as if he were going further. But they urged him strongly, 'Stay with us, for it is nearly evening; the day is almost over.' So he went in to stay with them.

When he was at the table with them he took bread, gave thanks, broke it and began to give it to them. Then their eyes were opened and they recognised him, and he disappeared from their sight. They asked each other, 'Were not our hearts burning within us while he talked with us on the road and opened the Scriptures to us?'
Luke 24:13-32

Reflection

Have you recognised Jesus on your journey?
How do you respond to the revelation of Jesus?

Prayer

Father God,
thank you that you walk with us through the days of our life.
Thank you that you are a God who explains and helps us to understand who you are.
Thank you that you are a God of revelation as well as information.
Amen.

Fifteen

Too good to be true?

My son prayed an amazing prayer this week.

'Jesus, please come into my heart.'

That was his prayer. I had no idea what had prompted him to pray it. We say prayers with him at night, he listens to Christian kids' videos and CDs, we read children's Bible stories and he goes to Sunday School. Now, I know that, after just writing all of that, it does sound rather a lot, but those are the things that he is exposed to; we as his parents do not sit him down and try to teach him theology or persuade him to become a Christian. We know he will have to make his own mind up and we want him to be sure, and to make his own decision, in his own time, when he is older.

Joseph is 5!

Did he really have any understanding of what he was saying?

The next day he suddenly looked up at me. He had been playing with his toys on the carpet one moment and the next second he was saying: 'Is Jesus in my heart?' His big eyes looked searchingly into mine. I could almost hear his thoughts: 'Come on, Dad, you are meant to know these things so just give me the answer, it's either a yes or a no, how difficult can this be for you?'

'Why did you say that prayer?' I asked my son. I didn't want to lead him with anything I said and, as this conversation had come years earlier than I had expected, I was definitely playing it by ear.

'Because I want him to live in my heart, but I don't want to hurt him!'

I tried to explain that Jesus living in our hearts doesn't hurt him and, if that is where Joseph really wanted Jesus to live, then he would.

The next day Claire told me that, on his way to school, Joseph had been telling people that Jesus lived in his heart.

We were thrilled and I was a little confused. Was Joseph a Christian now? Was that it? All of a sudden, out of the blue? If he had meant what he said . . .

Claire was 5 when she had become a Christian, and spent many Sunday evenings putting her hand up to the Gospel appeal until she finally 'felt' that she was a real Christian. Although she had to seriously think through what that decision meant as she grew up, she knew that she knew Jesus from a very early age.

We know that Joseph will have to think everything through for himself too, but why should we doubt the sincerity of a child's prayer or God's ability to discern and to act? Doubt and faith, two seemingly incompatible friends, and yet they often turn up together. One always ready to steal the other's thunder, always ready to step in and spoil the party or, alternatively, to let the banquet begin.

As we finish our reflections on this most dramatic of events we find a group of confused characters encountering Jesus. Once again I just love the honesty and humanity of these fellow humans. They see Jesus and they are startled. They see him and they can't believe what they are seeing! Who said seeing was believing? These men, these followers of Jesus, take some time to be convinced and realise the reality of the resurrection.

How about you? Have you grasped the meaning of the empty grave?

Have you had your eyes opened to the One who triumphed over death?

Have you allowed your doubts to meet with Jesus and watched them disappear?

Have you found yourself following this man who is God all the days of your life?

The disciples were witnesses and, if we know Jesus, we are witnesses too.

We don't have to wait until we are perfect or know all there is to know. Once we have met Jesus we have something to say and someone to share. A small group of people some two thousand years ago were so thrilled and excited at meeting the risen Jesus that they went out and, with God's help, they changed the world.

We can do the same today.

Bible reading

While they were still talking about this, Jesus himself stood among them and said to them, 'Peace be with you.'

They were startled and frightened, thinking they saw a ghost. He said to them, 'Why are you troubled, and why do doubts rise in your minds? Look at my hands and my feet. It is I myself! Touch me and see; a ghost does not have flesh and bones, as you see I have.'

When he had said this, he showed them his hands and feet. And while they still did not believe it because of joy and amazement, he asked them, 'Do you have anything here to eat?' They gave him a piece of broiled fish, and he took it and ate it in their presence.

He said to them, 'This is what I told you while I was still with you: Everything must be fulfilled that is written about me in the Law of Moses, the Prophets and the Psalms.'

Then he opened their minds so they could understand the Scriptures. He told them, 'This is what is written: The Christ will suffer and rise from the dead on the third day, and repentance and forgiveness of sins will be preached in his name to all nations, beginning at Jerusalem. You are witnesses of these things. I am going to send you what my Father has promised; but stay in the city until you have been clothed with power from on high.'
Luke 24:36-49

And on

Is it a bird?
Is it a plane?
Or is it Superman?
But what kind of a man? A good man?
A bad man?
Or a God man?
A preacher,
  a teacher,
  a breacher
  of life's final boundary;
  the defeater of death,
  the life that lives on,
  and on and on,
  one thousand years on.
Not hiding behind a mask,
  or identity disguised,
  nor lurking in the shadows,
  when he's the light of the world
  who shines on

and on and on,
two thousand years
on and on and . . .

Reflection

Do I doubt the reality of the resurrection?
What kind of a witness am I?

Prayer

Father God,
thank you for the Easter story, a wonderful, powerful, life-changing, life-enhancing story that is just as real today as when Jesus sat and ate a plate of fish with his first-century followers.
Amen.

Other titles by Tony Bower

1500412

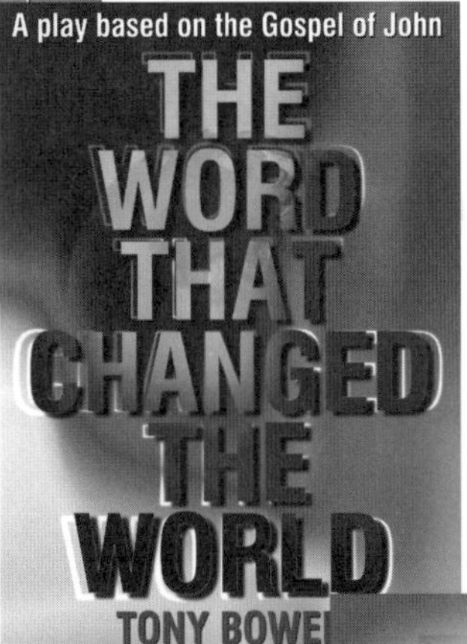

1500447

1500500